STEM IS EVERYWHERE

WHAT'S THAT SOUND?

JOHN LESLEY

REDBACK
publishing

Redback Publishing
PO Box 357 Frenchs Forest NSW 2086
Australia

www.redbackpublishing.com
orders@redbackpublishing.com

ISBN 978-1-922322-86-9

Author: John Lesley
Editor: Marlene Vaughn
Designer: Redback Publishing

Original illustrations © Redback Publishing 2022
Originated by Redback Publishing

Printed and bound in Malaysia

Acknowledgements
Abbreviations: l—left, r—right, b—bottom, t—top, c—centre, m—middle
We would like to thank the following for permission to reproduce
photographs: (Images © shutterstock) pg24m marcobrivio.photo /
Shutterstock.com

A catalogue record for this
book is available from the
National Library of Australia

CONTENTS

WHAT IS SOUND?

Have you ever wondered how sound gets from the place where it is made and travels to your ears, where you hear it?

Sound is not something you can see. This is because sound is a transfer of energy.

SOUND WAVES

Sound travels in waves and it needs some sort of matter to move through. Sound travels through the air, but it can also travel through a solid or a liquid.

If you like swimming, you have probably heard sounds underwater. If you put your ear against a wall in your home, you can often hear what is happening in the next room. All of these sounds happen because the sound wave is moving through matter.

VIBRATION

Matter vibrates when it moves back and forth quickly. If you hit a drum, this makes the drum surface vibrate. The energy of the vibration passes to the air around the drum, and is then transferred to molecule after molecule in the air until it eventually reaches your ears.

Waves in the ocean are a bit like sound waves. The wave energy travels over many kilometres through the molecules of water, but the water itself does not travel. A wave that causes water to crash onto a beach has started way out in the ocean.

In air, sound waves also travel, but the air itself does not go on the same journey. The air that transfers the sound into your ear is not the same air where the sound originated. Only the energy of that sound has reached you.

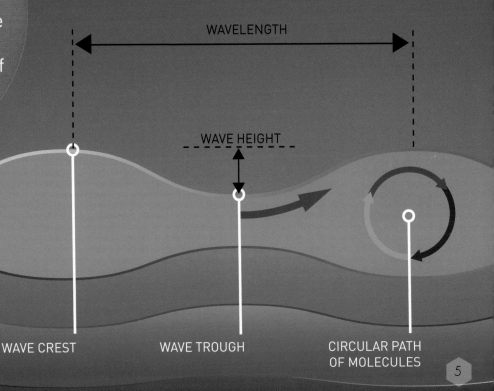

WAVELENGTH

WAVE HEIGHT

WAVE CREST

WAVE TROUGH

CIRCULAR PATH OF MOLECULES

TYPES OF SOUND

MOST OF US ARE SO USED TO HEARING SOUNDS THAT WE DON'T STOP TO THINK ABOUT WHAT THEY ARE.

NOISE

When we say that something is noisy, this usually means that we are hearing a jumble of different sorts of sound waves.

ANIMALS

Lots of animals make sounds to communicate. Pets even learn to make sounds so they can communicate with us. A smart cat will know the exact sound to make to tell us that it is hungry and wants its dinner.

MUSIC

SILENCE

Silence is an absence of sound waves. There is no vibration in the air near our ears when there is silence.

SPEAKING

When we speak, our mouth and throat make sounds that travel through the air to a listener. We move those parts of our body in very special ways to make particular sounds that have meaning to others.

VOCAL FOLDS

OPEN

CLOSED

VOCAL FOLDS

VOCAL FOLDS

EPIGLOTTIS

TRACHEA

WHAT'S IN YOUR THROAT?

MAKING MUSIC

People create musical instruments that control the way sound is produced.

The vibration of the musical instrument transfers to the air around it. This vibrating air becomes the sound we hear through our ears.

TYPES OF MUSICAL INSTRUMENTS

PERCUSSION INSTRUMENTS

Percussion instruments need to be hit to make sounds. These include drums and triangles. The enclosed part of the drum makes the sound louder.

PIANOS

In a piano, the keys are attached to strings of different lengths and thicknesses that vibrate to make various sounds as they are struck with a little hammer.

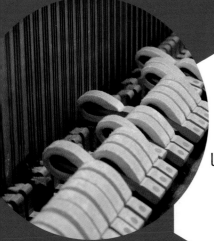

STRING INSTRUMENTS

String instruments include guitars and violins. When a string is plucked or bowed, it vibrates at a speed that depends on its length and thickness. When the player presses their fingers on the strings, it changes the length that can vibrate, which changes the sound.

WIND INSTRUMENTS

Wind instruments make air vibrate inside them as the player blows into or across the mouthpiece. A recorder sounds different as we place fingers over the holes, because this changes the sound wave we create. Didgeridoos, bamboo flutes and tubas are all wind instruments. Wind instruments include brass and woodwind.

HOW TO DESCRIBE A SOUND

Sound is so important for communication that we need many more words than just loud or soft to describe it. Scientists have special words that tell us all about the sound wave that is causing the sound.

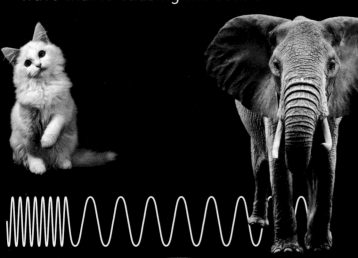

Many animals can hear sounds that we cannot. Dogs and cats can hear higher pitched sounds than us, but elephants can hear much lower pitched sounds.

FREQUENCY

The frequency of a sound is the number of times the sound wave vibrates in a second.

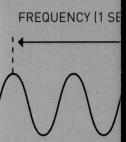

FREQUENCY (1 SE

LOUDNESS

Loudness determines how easy it is for us to hear a noise. Bigger sound waves carry louder sounds to our ears.

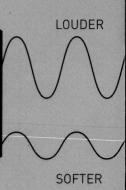

LOUDER

SOFTER

PITCH

The pitch of a sound is whether it sounds high or low. A mouse's squeak has a high pitch, but a big dog's bark has a low pitch. A high-pitched sound vibrates very quickly, and a low-pitched sound vibrates slowly.

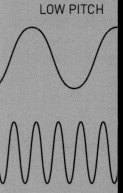

LOW PITCH

HIGH PITCH

DOPPLER EFFECT

As an ambulance passes you in the street with its siren blaring, the sound suddenly changes from being high to low-pitched.

LOW PITCH

HIGH PITCH

This is caused by the sound waves being pushed together in front of the moving ambulance. As it passes you, the siren sounds different because the sound waves are suddenly further apart.

HELIUM BALLOON VOICES

If you have ever heard a person speaking with a squeaky voice after breathing helium gas, you might have wondered how this happens. Sound travels faster in helium than it does in normal air. Through interacting with our voice production, the helium changes the way we sound.

TOO LOUD!

SOUND IN DECIBELS

30DB WHISPER

60DB TALKING

80DB MOTOR CARS

90DB LAWN MOWER

120DB LOUD CONCERT

140DB JET PLANE

FEELING A SOUND

We usually know a sound exists because we hear it with our ears, but there are also times when we feel a sound with our whole body.

All sounds are waves of pressure in the air. Very loud sounds strike us with a level of air pressure that can damage our ears, and which we feel throughout our body as an uncomfortable pressure.

LOUD MUSIC

Hearing very loud music at a concert or in earphones can damage the delicate parts of our ears. This can reduce our ability to hear perfectly later.

WORKING NEAR LOUD MACHINERY

People who have to use loud machinery in their jobs need to wear protective ear coverings. Constant exposure to loud sounds allows pressure waves to damage our ear drums and cause hearing loss.

TECHNOLOGY AND SOUND

Scientists and designers use technology to construct the inventions we need to make use of sound. Without their research and creativity, we would not have any of the devices we all depend on to talk to each other over long distances, or to enjoy movies, videos and television.

AMPLIFIERS

Amplifiers are used to make sounds louder. The large round part of an amplifier is called a loudspeaker. When it vibrates, it transfers energy to the air as a sound wave.

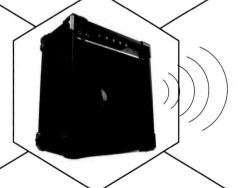

The loudspeakers used for music can be different depending on the pitch of the sound projected out of them. A subwoofer is good for producing low-pitched sounds, and a tweeter is better for high-pitched sounds.

TELEPHONES

Telephones were invented in the late 1800s. Before that time, a person had to write a letter to communicate with someone far away. People in some ancient societies used writing on clay tablets or on pieces of wood to send messages to each other.

MICROPHONES

Microphone technology first appeared in the late 1800s. The role of a microphone is to convert a sound wave into an electrical wave.

ELECTRICAL SIGNAL

SOUND WAVES

DIAPHRAGM

COILS

MAGNET

MAKE A MEGAPHONE

Make your own megaphone out of a large half-circle of cardboard. Roll it into a cone shape and then talk into the small hole at one end. Doing this will make your voice sound much louder.

EARS

Our ears are wonderful. They take sound vibrations around us and turn them into information that our brain decides is either music, annoying noise, words or a sign of danger.

6 The brain tells us we have heard something, and works out exactly what sort of sound it is.

1 Sound reaches the outer part of our ear and is funnelled into the ear canal by the soft parts called the pinna.

5 This nerve sends an electric pulse to the brain.

2 The sound wave presses on our tiny eardrum, making it vibrate.

3 The vibration is transferred to little bones inside the ear.

4 The sound energy reaches the hearing nerve.

PEOPLE WHO CANNOT HEAR SOUNDS

People who are deaf usually have a part of their ear that does not work. They still communicate excellently using a variety of methods

Learning to lip-read

Using a cochlear implant

Using a hearing aid placed in the ear canal

Using sign language with hand gestures

A B C D E F G H I J K L M N O P Q R S T U V W X Y Z

ECHOES

SOUND CAN BOUNCE!

An echo is sound that repeats itself by bouncing or reflecting back off a wall or other smooth, hard surface. You may be able to hear an echo in a very large room that has no carpets or furniture in it. Echoes also happen in large caves or valleys between high mountain walls.

Sound does not bounce off soft surfaces. Furniture and curtains in a room, or trees and grass in the outdoors, do not send echoes back to the sender.

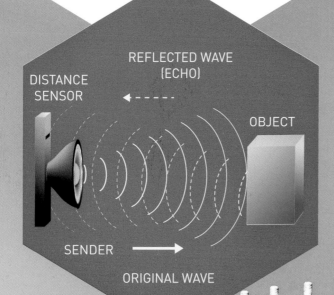

DISTANCE SENSOR

REFLECTED WAVE (ECHO)

OBJECT

SENDER

ORIGINAL WAVE

UNUSUAL PLACES IN THE WORLD TO HEAR ECHOES

TEMPLE OF HEAVEN, BEIJING
The curved Echo Wall around this building is able to transmit sounds.

ST PAUL'S CATHEDRAL, LONDON
The Whispering Wall is part of a circular gallery near the top of the dome. Visitors speaking quietly near the wall can be heard by someone right over on the opposite side.

ECHOLOCATION

Bats and dolphins use echolocation to work out what is in their surroundings. They both produce high-pitched squeaks and can measure the way the reflected sound comes back to them. This allows them to work out if they should avoid swimming or flying into something solid, or if there is food nearby. Bats can detect tiny insects using echolocation.

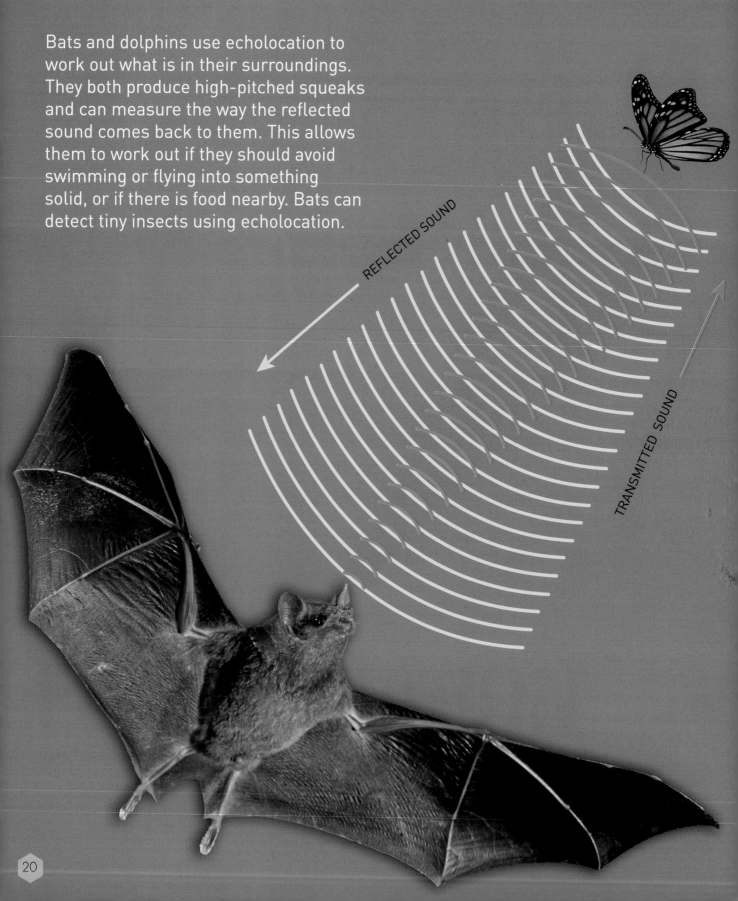

REFLECTED SOUND

TRANSMITTED SOUND

SONAR

Humans also use echolocation, but we use technology rather than our own bodies to read the reflected sounds.

Sonar is a method of sending out sound waves underwater. People who are fishing use the results to see if there are schools of fish under their boat.

Sonar is also used in defence force operations to see if there are submarines under the water.

SOUND IN MEDICINE

ULTRASOUND

Ultrasound is sound produced at very high frequency, far beyond the level that people can hear.

Health workers use ultrasound waves to see what is happening inside a sick person's body. Ultrasound images are also a safe way to see how a baby is growing inside its mother.

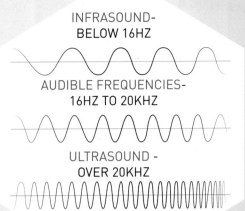

INFRASOUND- BELOW 16HZ

AUDIBLE FREQUENCIES- 16HZ TO 20KHZ

ULTRASOUND - OVER 20KHZ

Ultrasound works by sending sound waves at an object, then measuring the bounced waves as they come back to the machinery. These echoes are converted into images on a screen.

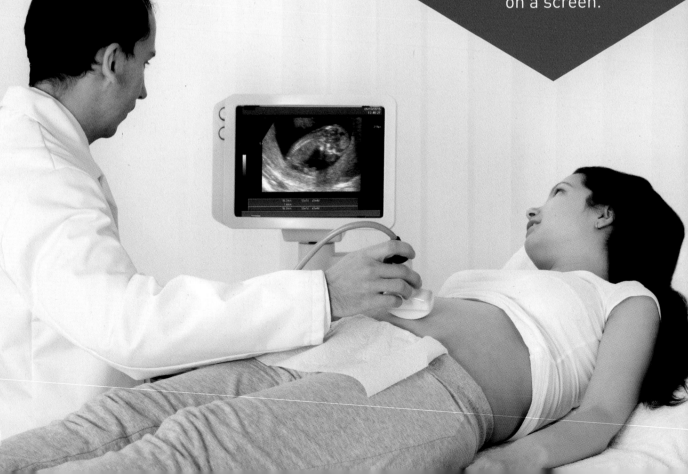

REVERBERATION

Sounds produced in enclosed places can sound louder because of reverberation. This is caused by the sound wave bouncing around inside the space.

Your voice sounds better when you sing in the shower because the glass and tiles on the walls cause the sound to reverberate, making your voice seem stronger than it really is.

TUNING FORK

SOUND WAVES

VIBRATING WATER

HOW TO MAKE A MOBILE PHONE SOUND LOUDER

Sit a mobile phone inside a bowl. When the phone rings, reverberation of the sound inside the bowl makes the ringing sound louder.

RESONANCE

Resonance happens when the vibrations of a sound make an object start to vibrate as well. If you strike a tuning fork and hold it near some water, the surface of the water will start to vibrate in resonance.

PLACES CHANGE SOUND

Why is sound inside a little room different from sound out on a mountain top or in an opera house?

If you listen to a singer inside a large concert hall, the sound is clear and easy to hear. If the same singer stands on a mountain top and sings, their voice does not sound the same.

In a well-designed concert hall, such as those in the Sydney Opera House, the walls and ceilings are all built so that the sound bounces off them in ways that do not cause echoes. The musical sounds we hear are clear and rich. Out in the open, singing is more difficult to hear.

RECORDING STUDIOS

Singers and musicians use studios to make recordings. The studio will often have padding on the walls, floor and ceiling. The people who design recording studios avoid having large, smooth surfaces that would cause the sound waves to bounce back off them, interfering with the music or singing.

NOISY CAR ENGINES

If we start a car engine inside a garage, the sound is very loud and uncomfortable to listen to. As soon as the car moves out into the open, the sound of its engine seems to be quieter. The engine is working in exactly the same way, so why does it sound different?

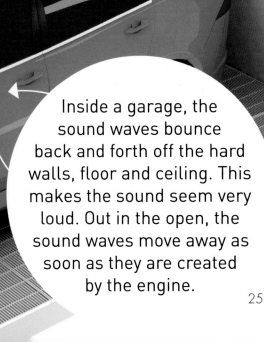

Inside a garage, the sound waves bounce back and forth off the hard walls, floor and ceiling. This makes the sound seem very loud. Out in the open, the sound waves move away as soon as they are created by the engine.

OUTER SPACE

Sound needs matter to travel. Because space is mostly a vacuum, with no matter in it, sound cannot travel through it.

Unlike sound, light is a form of energy that can travel across space. This is why we can see stars that are very far away. We can even see gigantic explosions occurring in other parts of the Universe. We cannot ever hear these explosions, because the sound they make has no way of travelling across the emptiness of space.

SOUND ON THE MOON

The Moon does not have an atmosphere. This means there are no gases to transfer vibrations. Astronauts who walked on the Moon could not shout at each other through their helmets since there was no air to carry the sounds they made. They had to use radio communication to talk to each other.

NO AIR OUTSIDE = NO SOUND

AIR INSIDE = SOUND

Out in space, astronauts might be able hear each other if they press their helmets together. The sound they make inside their helmet could then travel as a vibration through to the air inside their fellow astronaut's helmet.

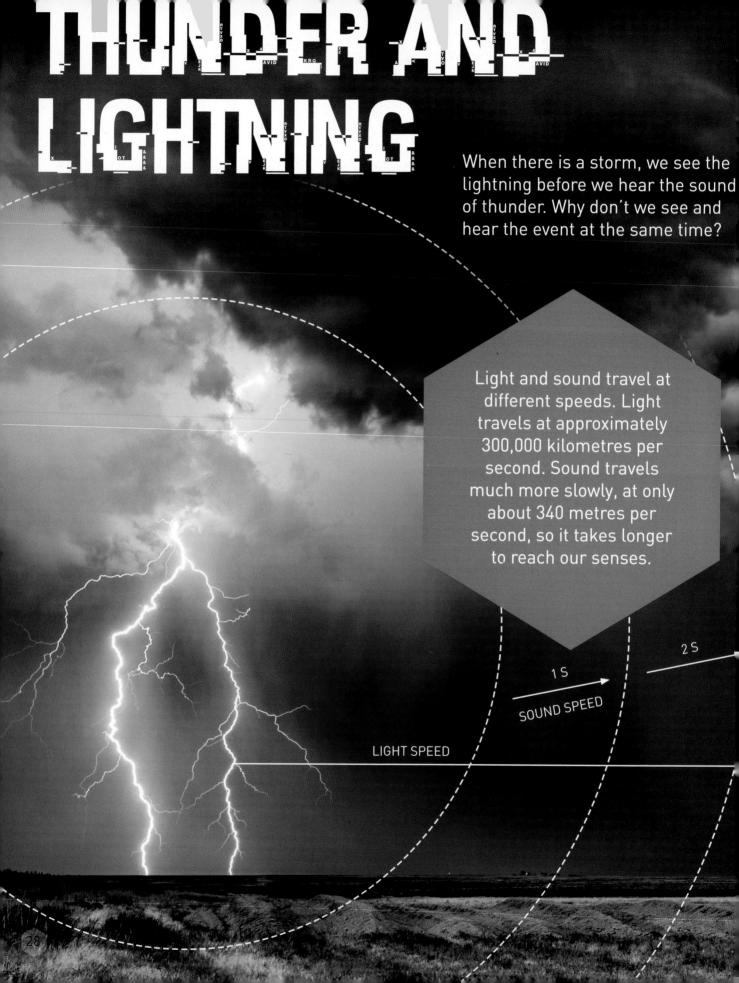

THUNDER AND LIGHTNING

When there is a storm, we see the lightning before we hear the sound of thunder. Why don't we see and hear the event at the same time?

Light and sound travel at different speeds. Light travels at approximately 300,000 kilometres per second. Sound travels much more slowly, at only about 340 metres per second, so it takes longer to reach our senses.

2 S

1 S

SOUND SPEED

LIGHT SPEED

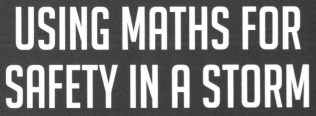

USING MATHS FOR SAFETY IN A STORM

We can guess how far away a storm is by measuring the time between when we see the lightning and when we hear the thunder from it. If the difference is three seconds, then the storm is about a kilometre away.

Using this simple maths is a good way to keep safe. If we know the storm is a few kilometres away, then we know we have time to get safely indoors before the lightning comes too near us.

3 SECONDS:
1 KM AWAY

6 SECONDS:
2 KM AWAY

4 S

5 S

6 S

7 S

NOISE POLLUTION

Pollution in the environment extends beyond adding dangerous chemical substances to the air, water and soil. Pollution can also be in the form of unwanted sound waves.

LOUD NOISES

Loud noises from machinery, thunder, music or shouting can all be polluting. They upset some people and make the environment unpleasant. Very loud noises can damage a person's ears.

NOISES FROM WIND FARMS

Some people say that the noise of windmills in wind farms makes them feel ill.

WILDLIFE

Unusual noises can disturb wild animals. In Australia, some government authorities have used noise to make wild fruit bats leave areas that are close to where people work and live.

WORDS ABOUT SOUND

amplifier	electronic device that makes sound louder
decibel	measurement of loudness
Doppler Effect	change in pitch heard as a moving sound passes us
echolocation	finding objects using reflected sound
matter	substances
megaphone	funnel shaped object for making voice louder
molecule	tiny particle making up matter
pinna	external, soft part of ear
pitch	whether a sound is high or low
resonance	ability of an object to vibrate due to sound waves
reverberation	repeated sound wave
sonar	technology for finding objects underwater using sound
ultrasound	very high frequency sound
vacuum	space with no matter in it
vibration	rapid back and forth movement

INDEX